Making a Woven

John Boakes

Smith
Settle

First published in 2001 by
Smith Settle Ltd
Ilkley Road
Otley
West Yorkshire
LS21 3JP

ISBN 1 85825 117 6

British Library Cataloguing-in-Publication data:
A catalogue record for this book is available from the British Library.

Set in Monotype Plantin

Designed, printed and bound by
SMITH SETTLE
Ilkley Road, Otley, West Yorkshire LS21 3JP

Introduction

For centuries, hurdle-making was nearly always a family trade, and it was not unusual for three generations of one family to work side by side. In this way the skills were passed on from father to son. It was usual for each little family group of craftsmen to make hurdles for all the surrounding farms within a ten or twelve mile (16-19km) radius of the woods where they worked, and these hurdles were very rarely sold outside of this area. Unfortunately, today the modern hurdle-makers normally have to sell their wares to a market much further afield.

Owners of some of the larger farms would take the trouble to plant their own woodland areas, so that all their own farm's needs could be met. This type of woodland was called 'coppiced', from the French *couper*, to cut. The cut woodland was carefully managed by allowing some of the larger trees to grow normally, usually spaced about thirty to forty feet (9-12m) apart, which provided a habitat for the cut hazel, willow, chestnut and ash to grow unimpeded towards the canopy. This then produced good straight wood for use in such items as hurdles, sticks for shepherds' crooks and handles for tools, as well as many other implements important in the running of the farm. Also, this type of environment provided the required conditions for rare plants and butterflies such as the heath fritillary, purple emperor, chequered skipper and wood white to flourish. Unfortunately, though, because most of these woodlands have not been coppiced for the last fifty years, these species have now become very rare.

Until the 1950s, coppiced woodlands would have been worked by several groups of different craftsmen, one such being the hurdle-makers. That is not so today, for these coppiced woods have all but disappeared as a working enviroment, and most of the crafts pursued in them have also ceased as a full-time payable proposition. Hurdles, for example, were once needed in their hundreds, but today, with the introduction of electric and moveable metal fences, the need for them has virtually gone. But a few dedicated craftsmen have tried to preserve these skills, more for their own enjoyment as a hobby, or even in some cases as part-time employment. Also, there are now a few of these new craftsmen managing to combine hurdle-making with some of the other country crafts, such as hedging, walling and fencing, so that they can make a full-time living.

The average working life of a hurdle was usually anything between five and seven years, and a good hurdle-maker could make at least 1,800 a year. Before the First World War, this same hurdle-maker could sell his hurdles for £1 4s (£1.20) to £1 10s (£1.50) a dozen. Nowadays, the small number of hurdle-makers still left can sell an average four foot (1.2m) hurdle for around £25.

There have always been two different kinds of hurdle, usually made in different parts of the country. Both are designed to do the same jobs — to be used as a portable fence to secure livestock, as well as as a stop-gap to repair broken gates and field fences. The hurdles varied in size from county to county, being anything between 5 and 10 feet (1.5-3m) long and 3½ to 4½ feet (1-1.3m) high. The smallest were usually made in Norfolk and East Anglia, and a good Norfolk hurdle-maker could make up to three hurdles in an hour, these being sold about fifty years ago for around 5s 9d (29p) a dozen.

Of the two different types of hurdle, the *wattle* was the most popular. The wattle hurdle, usually made in the South, is a woven type, using either split or in some cases thin, under one inch (25mm) thick, flexible lengths, such as the willow hurdles of Somerset and Norfolk. A finished wattle hurdle gives a light, solid, impenetrable barrier, and was used to provide a windbreak and safe shelter for young lambs in the spring. A farm with approximately 700 sheep would have at least 100 hurdles in constant use, and a percentage of these would need to be replaced every year. Secondly, there is the bar type, which looks like a portable five-bar gate. Being the stronger of the two, this could also be used with larger animals such as cows. It is usually made from cleft chestnut, and was the most widely used type in the North, where it was called a *riven* hurdle. This refers to the type of wood used in its manufacture, 'riven' being another name for split or cleft.

Hurdles were also used for other purposes. Seaside towns bought them in great numbers to be used on the beaches by holidaymakers as windbreaks, but with the introduction of the modern, cheaper, gaily coloured canvas windbreaks, the old-fashioned hurdles were not needed any more. However, the hurdle is still to be seen at race courses up and down the country, being used as barriers in the many hurdle races at National Hunt meetings. The wattle hurdle has also been given a new lease of life by its fashionable popularity in modern-day gardening, where it is used as a fence or barrier. Thanks to this, it is now possible to buy them up and down the country in garden centres.

Hopefully, this intrinsically beautiful craftsman-made product, with so many uses in the past, will continue to be made for a good few years to come. Today, one of those still making this product is Dan Watson in his workshop and yard not far from the tiny village of Thorner in West Yorkshire. Dan was taught the craft of hurdle-making in Devon by one of the best hurdle-makers in the country, Herbert Snowdon, after which, with help from the Prince's Trust, he set up in business on his own over eight years ago. But like most country crafts, hurdle-making is seasonal, and it takes up only part of Dan's working year; at other times he is involved in charcoal making, rustic furniture, hedging, walling and coppicing. In this book we see Dan making a hurdle from split hazel.

Bibliography

Alan Brookes (revised by Elizabeth Agate), *Hedging: a practical handbook* (1975 & 1976).
Herbert L Edlin, *Woodland Craft of Britain* (1949 & 1973).
H E Fitzrandolph & M D Hay, *The Rural Crafts of England and Wales* (1926 & 1977).
J E Manners, *Woodland Crafts Today* (1974).

Acknowledgments

The author would like to thank: Dan Watson, hurdle-maker of Thorner, West Yorkshire; Peter Holmes of Harrogate; Nicola Mills of the Beamish Photographic Library for the use of the photographs on pages 8-9; and Caroline Benson of the Rural History Centre at the university of Reading for the photographs on pages 12-13, 16, 39, 46.

A pile of finished hurdles at Dan Watson's workshop in West Yorkshire, waiting to go out to a customer.

An 1881 engraving showing hurdle makers at work.

A man fastening a riven hurdle across the broken part of a drystone wall to serve as a stop-gap.

Coppiced hazel waiting to be used, in the yard of Dan Watson's workshop.

(Left) First, Dan cuts the upright poles or *sails* with a side axe to the required length. *(Centre)* Those that are too thick are split with a billhook, ensuring that the cut runs along the grain. *(Right)* Then the sails are pointed at one end.

(This page)
One-time hurdle maker Mr J Heath of Leamington Spa pointing off one of the sails of a wattle hurdle in the 1950s.

(Facing page)
A hurdle maker clearing the mortice in a gate or riven hurdle.

Dan's *sett board*, with the holes already drilled out to the required distance apart. This ensures that every hurdle is the same size.

He then puts the sails in position. The two thickest are placed at the ends to give strength.

An old photo of a wattle hurdle with ten sails fitted into place. You can see the stack of finished hurdles in the background.

Dan cuts the *rods* for the weaving to a uniform length.

(Clockwise from top left) The rods are split along the grain using the billhook, by making a downwards cut a few inches from one end; this cut goes about half way into the rod. Then the billhook is used to ease the cut along the rod, ensuring that the grain is followed. If this is done properly, the split follows the grain around any blemishes in the rod. The two halves of the split rods are laid out side by side on a rest; they are always used in order.

The two *locking rods* are first laid into position at each end. These are used later to secure the wattle into place.

Dan weaves the first rod between the sails. These first few rods are always unsplit.

The bottom rod is always twisted around the outside sail twice to secure the bottom of the hurdle. This will also be done at the top of the hurdle as well.

The bottom rod in position, with the two locking rods also visible.

The bottom six rods are woven into position.

The bottom locking rod is twisted around the end sail and woven back along the top of the weaving already completed.

The locking rod in position.

The bottom part of the weaving is now complete.

The first split hazel rod is then woven in. These rods are traditionally always put in the hurdle the same way around.

The first split rod in position.

Dan hammers the split rods tight with a wooden mallet. These mallets were traditionally made in the woods by the hurdle-makers.

(Top) The hurdle is about one third finished. *(Bottom)* The other side of the hurdle, showing the darker bark side.

Where the rods are not long enough to be woven into the hurdle again, they are left protruding as each section is finished.

As each section is finished, the excess is cut off level with the end sail.

The last of the split rods is woven into the hurdle.

The hurdle is levelled, allowing enough space for the top band of rods to be woven into place.

The top locking rods are first to be put on.

Then the last few unsplit rods are woven in, each one carefully twisted around the end sail.

When using the thinner pieces of hazel, Dan must be very careful to ensure that the rod does not break.

Dan double-twists the locking rod around the end sail and it is then woven back into the hurdle.

Mr C Glasspool of Sussex about to finish a split-hazel hurdle.

Dan uses the billhook when weaving the locking rod back into the hurdle.

He gives the hurdle a last hammering to tighten everything up.

Finally, any pieces still sticking out are cut off.

Dan's shelter is made from the material close at hand, and is not unlike the *bodger's hovel* once seen in centuries past. (A bodger was a man who lived and worked in the woods, using freshly cut unseasoned wood to produce all manner of household ware.)

The tools that Dan uses.

Dan's home-made *horse*,
ready for use.

(Above) Mr Kinnard of West Sussex and his assistant work as a team making wattle hurdles in the 1940s-50s.

(Facing page) Dan proudly shows us the finished hurdle